Our
Iceberg
Is Melting

What People Are Saying

"*Our Iceberg Is Melting* is superb. It embodies powerful messages that can help a broad audience. It covers all the steps to success in a changing world, from finding the substantial issues, aligning with a potent champion, charting the course, getting buy-in, dealing with those who want no change, and so on."

—Chris Hand, Citigroup Global Account
Vice President, Avaya Corporation

"Never have I read a parable in a business book that took a complex issue like change management and distilled it down into a simple story for all to understand. This is the ideal follow-on to *Leading Change* and *The Heart of Change*. A must-read for anyone dealing with managing change."

—Richard J. Kosinski, Category
Development Officer, Yahoo Inc.

"Our *Iceberg Is Melting* is fantastic—offbeat, but right on. We should make everyone in Washington, DC, read it."

—John Batten, Executive Vice President, Twin Disc Inc.

"I came across *Our Iceberg Is Melting* in May, ordered and distributed sixty copies in June, evaluated its effect on our change effort, and then ordered five hundred more copies in September. This is a gem."

—Heidi King, Program Manager, U.S. Department of Defense

"This is the easiest-to-read yet most informative book I have ever seen. Setting one of management's biggest challenges—'What problem? I don't see a problem'—in the context of a melting iceberg and a determined penguin was a stroke of sheer genius."

—Michael Dimelow, Director, Product Marketing,
TTP Communications PLC

"I have followed Kotter's work for years, respect it greatly, use it with my clients, and know its unique power to help people and organizations perform better. This latest effort—this little penguin tale—is, in my opinion, the best and most useful book he has ever written."

—Alan Frohman, President, Frohman Associates

"As a result of the book and my sharing it with a few people in the organization, we have moved quickly on several fronts. We are galvanized to go ahead instead of further studying, more organizing, and so on. It is making a difference for us."

—Tom Curley, President and CEO, Associated Press

"It's a great book. It does an excellent job of communicating in a simple and humorous way the key challenges of leading change. We can easily identify with the characters. It allows a lighthearted discussion of very difficult issues."

—Deb Karstetter, Executive Vice President,
ABD Insurance & Financial Services

"When I was a child in France, I was first introduced to the French classic *The Little Prince*. I reread this marvelous book while in college and many times since as an adult. It is a book that keeps me growing and thinking. I can see *Our Iceberg Is Melting* becoming *The Little Prince* for the twenty-first century."

—Stephan Bancel, General Manager, Eli Lilly, Belgium

"My fifteen-year-old daughter saw me reading *Our Iceberg Is Melting*, and when I left the book in the den, she began to read it. When she was done, my wife read it. Afterward, we all talked about it. What I suspect will happen with our family, and especially with our daughter, is that we now have a referent story to use, one that's easy to remember and visually salient, when we discuss issues about change. It has 'stickiness' in that it's hard to forget."

—Peter Z. Orton, PhD, Program Director, Special
Projects, IBM On Demand Learning

"In this fast-paced world, with piles of data and written material, this book is a breath of fresh air. It is simple and to the point, easy to read, and filled with many ideas that we can all apply. I found my mind reflecting on the past on one page and thinking about the future on the next."

—Edward Day, Executive Vice President,
Southern Company Generation

Our Iceberg Is Melting

Changing and Succeeding Under Any Conditions

10th Anniversary Edition

John Kotter

and Holger Rathgeber

with artwork by Rebecca Solow

PORTFOLIO / PENGUIN

PORTFOLIO / PENGUIN
An imprint of Penguin Random House LLC
375 Hudson Street
New York, New York 10014

Most Portfolio books are available at a discount when purchased in quantity for sales promotions or corporate use. Special editions, which include personalized covers, excerpts, and corporate imprints, can be created when purchased in large quantities. For more information, please call (212) 572-2232 or e-mail specialmarkets@penguinrandomhouse.com. Your local bookstore can also assist with discounted bulk purchases using the Penguin Random House corporate Business-to-Business program. For assistance in locating a participating retailer, e-mail B2B@penguinrandomhouse.com.

Originally published by St. Martin's Press

Library of Congress Cataloging-in-Publication Data
Names: Kotter, John P., 1947– author. | Rathgeber, Holger, author.
Title: Our iceberg is melting : changing and succeeding under any conditions / John Kotter, Holger Rathgeber.
Description: New edition. | New York : Portfolio, 2016. | "First published in the United States by John Kotter and Holger Rathgeber under the title *Our Iceberg Is Melting: Changing and Succeeding Under Adverse Conditions.*" | Revised edition of the authors' Our iceberg is melting, 2006.
Identifiers: LCCN 2015040526 (print) | LCCN 2015047717 (ebook) | ISBN 9780399563911 (hardback) | ISBN 9780399563928 (ebook)
Subjects: LCSH: Organizational change. | Organizational effectiveness. | Penguins—Fiction. | BISAC: BUSINESS & ECONOMICS / Leadership. | BUSINESS & ECONOMICS / Motivational. | BUSINESS & ECONOMICS / Management.
Classification: LCC HD58.8 .K672 2016 (print) | LCC HD58.8 (ebook) | DDC 650.1—dc23
LC record available at http://lccn.loc.gov/2015040526

Printed in the United States of America
5 7 9 10 8 6 4

Book design by Cassandra Garruzzo

Foreword

Spencer Johnson, MD

Author of *Who Moved My Cheese?*

Coauthor of *The One Minute Manager*

On the surface, this wonderful book appears to be a simple fable that is easy to read and understand. But that is just the tip of the proverbial iceberg.

Working with John Kotter, at the Harvard Business School, I learned that he knows more about changing organizations than anyone, anywhere. Leaders and managers around the world have read his highly respected book, *Leading Change*, and have discovered that using his Eight Steps is the best way to ensure a successful organizational change.

What does that have to do with most of us?

Well, with *Our Iceberg Is Melting*, everyone working in any kind of organization—and that is most people—can now discover how to use the same Eight Steps, and enjoy more success in these changing times.

Professor Kotter and his equally creative coauthor, Holger Rathgeber, let us see how a group of penguins, in adverse conditions, use the steps, seemingly without knowing it.

Whether you work in a business, or the business of life, everyone from CEOs to high school students can gain from what each takes from this story.

As you enjoy reading what follows, you may want to ask yourself, "What is my 'iceberg,' and how can I use what I discover in the story?"

And then consider sharing it with others you work with. After all, things usually turn out better when everyone is on the same page.

Our
Iceberg
Is Melting

Welcome

Handle the challenge of change well, and you can prosper greatly. Handle it poorly, and you put yourself and others at risk.

All too often people and organizations don't see the need for change. They don't correctly identify what to do, or successfully make it happen, or make it stick. Businesses don't. School systems don't. Nations don't.

We have studied the challenge of change for decades. We know the traps into which even very smart people fall. We know the steps that can assure group success. And we will show you what we have found.

Our method is showing, much more than telling, and with the method that has helped more people learn over the centuries than any other single technique: the fable.

Fables can be powerful because they take serious, confusing, and threatening subjects and make them clear and approachable. Fables can be memorable, unlike so much of the information that bombards us today and is forgotten tomorrow. They can stimulate thought, teach important lessons, and motivate anyone—young or old—to use those lessons. In our modern, high-tech world, we can easily forget this simple yet profound truth.

If you know much about the setting in which we have placed our story—Antarctica—you'll see that life for our penguins is not exactly as you would find it on a National Geographic documentary. Fables are like that. If you think a fun story with illustrations must be for young children, you'll soon see this book is about real-life problems that frustrate nearly everyone in organizations.

The fable that follows was inspired by John Kotter's

award-winning research on how successful change really happens. All of us encounter the basic issues in the story. Few of us encounter highly effective ways of dealing well with those issues. And this is what our story is all about.

Our Iceberg Will Never Melt

O nce upon a time a colony of penguins was living in the frozen Antarctic on an iceberg near what we call today Cape Washington.

The iceberg had been there for many, many years. It was surrounded by a sea rich in food. On its surface were huge walls of eternal snow that gave penguins shelter from dreadful winter storms.

As far back as any of the penguins could remember,

they had always lived on that iceberg. "This is our home," they would tell you if you could ever find their world of ice and snow. They would also say, quite logically from their perspective, "And this will always be our home."

Where they lived, a waste of energy kills. Everyone in the colony knew they needed to huddle together to survive. So they had learned to depend on each other. They often behaved like a big family (which, of course, can be both good and bad).

The birds were truly beautiful. Called emperor penguins, they were the largest of seventeen types of Antarctic animals that seem perpetually to wear tuxedos.

Two hundred sixty-eight penguins lived in the colony. One of them was Fred.

Fred looked and acted much like the others. You would probably describe him as either "cute" or "dignified," unless you really dislike animals. But Fred was different from most penguins in one very important way.

This is Fred. He is watching the sea.

Fred was unusually curious and observant.

Other penguins went hunting for creatures in the sea—quite necessary, since there was no other food in Antarctica. Fred fished less and studied the iceberg and the sea more.

Other penguins spent much of their time with friends and relatives. Fred was a good husband and father, but he socialized less than average. He frequently went off by himself to take notes on what he had observed.

You might think that Fred was an odd bird, perhaps the sort of penguin that others did not want to spend time with. But that wasn't really true. Fred was just doing what seemed right to him. As a result, he was becoming increasingly alarmed by what he saw.

Fred had a briefcase stuffed full of observations, ideas, and conclusions. (Yes, a briefcase. This is a fable.) The information was increasingly disturbing. The information was beginning to cry out . . .

The Iceberg Is Melting and Might Break Apart Soon!

An iceberg that suddenly collapsed into many pieces would be a disaster for the penguins, especially if it occurred during the winter in a storm. Many of the older and younger birds would surely die. Who could say what all the consequences would be? Like all unthinkable events, there was no plan for how to deal with such a catastrophe.

Fred did not panic easily. But the more he studied his observations, the more he became unnerved.

Fred knew he had to do something. But he was in no position to make any pronouncements or dictate how others should act. He was not one of the leaders of the colony. He wasn't even a son, brother, or father of one of the leaders of the colony. And he had no track record as a credible iceberg forecaster.

Fred also remembered how fellow penguin Harold had been treated when he once suggested that their home was becoming more fragile. When no one seemed interested, Harold tried to assemble some evidence. His efforts were greeted with:

"Harold, you really do worry too much. Have a squid, you'll feel better."

"Fragile?! Jump up and down, Harold. Have fifty of us jump up and down at the same time. Does anything happen? Huh?"

"Your observations are fascinating, Harold. But they can be interpreted in four very different ways. You see, if one makes the assumption . . ."

Some birds said nothing, but they began to treat Harold differently. The change was subtle, but Fred had seen it. It was definitely not a change for the better.

Fred found himself feeling rather lonely.

What Do I Do Now?

The colony had a Leadership Council. It was also called the Group of Ten, led by the Head Penguin. (The teenagers had a different name for the group, but that's another story.)

Alice was one of the ten bosses. She was a tough, practical bird who had a reputation for getting things done. She was also close to the colony, unlike a few of her peers who were more aloof. Actually all of their breed of penguins look a bit aloof, but they don't all behave that way.

Fred decided that Alice would be less likely to dismiss his story than other more senior penguins. So he went to see her. Alice being Alice, he did not have to schedule an appointment.

Fred told her of his studies and his conclusions. She listened carefully, even though, frankly, she wondered if

Fred was having some sort of personal crisis. Problems with the wife? Eating too much squid with high mercury levels?

But . . . Alice being Alice, she did not ignore Fred. Instead, she said, skeptically, "Take me to the place that you think most clearly shows the problem."

That "place" was not on the upper surface of the iceberg, where the melting and its consequences were hard to see, but underneath and inside. Fred explained this to Alice. She listened, and not being the most patient of birds, said, "Fine, fine, fine. Let's go."

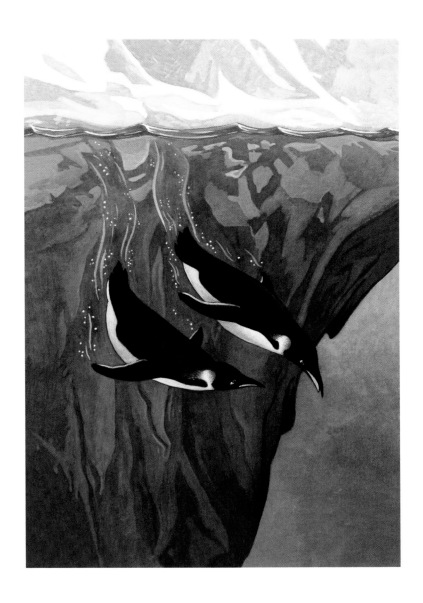

Penguins are vulnerable when they leap into the water because leopard seals and killer whales hide to catch careless birds. Without going into any unpleasant graphic detail, let's just say that you really don't want to be caught by a killer whale or leopard seal. So when Fred and Alice jumped into the sea, they were instinctively careful.

Below the surface, Fred pointed out fissures and other clear symptoms of deterioration caused by melting. Alice was amazed at how she had managed to ignore these signs.

Alice continued to follow Fred as he turned into a large hole at a sidewall of the iceberg. Through a canal a few meters wide, they swam deep into the heart of the ice, eventually reaching a spacious cave filled with water.

Alice tried to look as if she totally understood what she was seeing, but leadership was her specialty, not the science of icebergs. Fred saw the perplexed look. So when they returned to the surface, he explained.

To make a long story short—

Icebergs are not like ice cubes. The bergs can have cracks inside called canals. The canals can lead to large air bubbles called caves. If the ice melts sufficiently, cracks can be exposed to water, which would then pour into the canals and caves.

During a cold winter, the narrow canals filled with water can freeze quickly, trapping water inside the caves. But as the temperature goes lower and lower, the water in the caves will also freeze. Because a freezing liquid dramatically expands in volume, an iceberg could be broken into pieces.

After a few minutes, Alice began to see why Fred was so deeply concerned. The magnitude of the problem could be . . . ?

This was most definitely not good.

Alice was shaken, though she didn't show it. Instead, she asked Fred question after question.

"I need to think about what I've seen," she told him, "and then quickly talk with a few of my fellow leaders." Her mind was already plotting away.

"I will need your assistance," she told Fred. "I need you to be prepared to help others see and feel the problem." After a short pause, she added, "And be prepared that some birds won't want to see any problem."

Alice bid Fred good-bye. Fred felt both better and worse.

Better: He was no longer the only penguin who saw the potential for disaster. He wasn't the only penguin who felt a sense of urgency to do something about the problem.

Worse: He did not yet see any solution. And he did not much like the way Alice had said "be prepared" and "some birds won't want to see any problem."

The awful Antarctic winter was only two months away.

Problem? What Problem?

During the next few days, Alice contacted all members of the Leadership Council, including Louis, the Head Penguin. She asked them to go on the journey she had taken with Fred. Most listened to her. But they were very skeptical. Was Alice having a personal problem, perhaps with her marriage?!

None of those with whom Alice spoke showed any enthusiasm about the idea of swimming into a big dark cave. A few Council members could not even find time to see Alice. They said that they were busy with other important matters. They were dealing with a complaint from a rather loud bird that another penguin was making faces behind his back (a somewhat confusing issue since penguins cannot make faces).

They were also debating whether their weekly meetings should last two or two-and-a-half hours, a hot issue for those who liked jabbering and those who did not.

Alice asked Louis, the Head Penguin, to invite Fred to the next Leadership Council meeting to present and defend his conclusions. "After what you have told me about him, I am certainly very interested in hearing what Fred has to say," the Head Penguin said—diplomatically.

Louis did not, however, schedule time for a presentation by this relatively unknown penguin who had never before spoken to the group of leaders. But Alice was insistent, reminding her boss that they had to take some risks, "which you have bravely done all your life." That was true, more or less, and Louis was flattered to hear Alice say so (even though her motives were pretty obvious).

The Head Penguin agreed to invite Fred. Alice did.

In preparation for his meeting with the leaders, Fred considered writing a speech in which he would give statistics about the shrinking size of their home, the canals, the caves filled with water, the number of fissures obviously caused by melting, and so on. But when he asked a few of the older members of the colony about the Group of Ten, he learned that:

- Two of the birds on the Leadership Council loved to debate the validity of any statistics. And they loved to debate for hours and hours and hours and hours. These two were the more vocal advocates lobbying for longer meetings.
- One of the Leadership Council members would usually fall asleep—or at least come awfully close—during a long presentation with statistics. His snoring could be disruptive.
- Another bird was very uncomfortable with numbers. He tried to hide his feelings, usually by nodding his head a great deal. All the head

nodding tended to annoy some other members of the group, which could lead to bad moods and bickering.

- At least two other Council members made it pretty clear that they did not like to be *told* much of anything. They saw it as their job to be doing the *telling*.

After much thought, Fred chose an approach to the upcoming meeting that was different from his original plan.

Fred constructed a model of their iceberg. It was four feet by five feet and made of real ice and snow. The construction was not easy for Fred (especially since he had no hands, fingers, or opposable thumbs).

When he was done, Fred knew it was not perfect. But Alice thought it was a very creative idea and definitely good enough to help the leaders begin to see the problem.

The night before the meeting, Fred and his friends moved the model to where the leadership team met, which, unfortunately, was on the highest mountain of the iceberg. Halfway up the hill, the grumbling began. "Remind me why I'm doing this" was one of the kinder comments from his friends.

If penguins could grunt and groan, there would have been plenty of both.

The next morning, the leaders were already standing around the model when Fred arrived. Some were engaged in a lively debate. Others looked mystified.

Alice introduced Fred to the group.

Louis started the meeting, as the Head Penguin always did. "Fred, we want to hear about your discovery." Fred bowed respectfully. He could sense openness from Louis and some members of the group. Others seemed neutral. A few made little effort to hide their annoyance at having to listen to this so-called discovery.

Fred gathered his thoughts—and courage—and then told the story of his discovery. He explained the methods he had devised to study their home. He described how he had found the deterioration, the open canals, the big exposed cave full of water—all of which had to be caused by melting.

Constantly Fred used the model to orient his audience and illustrate his points. All but one of the Leadership Council penguins moved closer to the model.

When Fred removed the top half of the structure to show the big cave and explain its disastrous impact, you could have heard a snowflake falling on the ground.

When the demonstration was completed, there was silence.

Alice started the discussion by saying, "I saw all this with my own eyes. The cave full of water is huge. It's scary. I saw all the other signs of destruction that must be caused by the melting. We cannot ignore this anymore!"

A few penguins nodded.

One of the Leadership Council members was an older, heavyset bird named NoNo. NoNo was responsible for weather forecasting. There were two theories as to the origin of his name. One was that his great-grandfather had been called NoNo. Another theory was that his first words as a baby penguin were not "Ma" or "Pa," but "No, No."

NoNo was accustomed to being blamed for being wrong in his weather forecasts, but this business about the iceberg melting was too much for him. He spoke up, barely able to control his emotions. "I have regularly reported to this group about my observations of the climate and its effect on our iceberg," he said. "As I have told you before, periods of melting during warm summers are common. During winter, everything returns to normal. What he saw, or *thinks* he saw, is nothing new. There is no reason to worry! Our iceberg is solid and strong, and can withstand such fluctuations!"

Each sentence from NoNo came out louder than the last. If penguins could become red-faced, which they can't, he would have been red-faced.

When NoNo saw that the support of some of the others was turning in his favor, he pointed to Fred and said dramatically:

"This *junior* bird says melting ice has opened that canal. *But maybe it hasn't.* He says the canal will freeze this winter and trap the water in a big cave. *But maybe it won't!* He says the water in the cave will freeze. *But maybe it will not!* He says freezing water always expands in volume. *But maybe he's wrong!* And even if all he says turns out to be true, is our iceberg really so fragile that freezing water in a cave can break it into dangerously small pieces? *How do we know what he says is not just—a theory? Wild speculation? Fear mongering?!*"

NoNo paused, glared at the others, and threw what he hoped was a knock-out punch:

"Can he guarantee that his data and conclusions are *100 percent accurate?*"

Four of the birds nodded. One seemed to have become as mad as NoNo.

Alice quietly shot Fred an encouraging look that basically said: things are fine (which she knew was not true), you can handle this (which was not at all clear), now just go ahead and reply calmly (which for her would have been difficult since she wanted to scream, "NoNo, you nitwit!").

Fred said nothing. Alice gave him another encouraging look.

Fred hesitated, then said, "Honestly, no. I cannot give you a guarantee. No, I am not 100 percent sure. But should our melting iceberg break into many pieces, it will be in winter, when it is dark both day and night, when the terrible storms and winds make us most vulnerable. Wouldn't many, many of us die?"

Two of the birds standing near Fred seemed horrified. He looked in their direction and said, "Wouldn't it happen?"

Seeing that most of the Leadership Council still appeared to be very skeptical, Alice gave NoNo a hard look and said: "Imagine parents who lost their children. Imagine them coming to us and asking, 'How could this have happened? What were you doing? Why didn't you foresee this crisis? It was your job to protect the colony!' What would you tell them? 'Well, yes, sorry. We had heard that there might be a problem, but the information was not 100 percent credible.'"

She paused to let her comments sink in.

"What would we tell them as they stood before us in unspeakable pain? That we had *hoped* such a tragedy would not happen? That it was not appropriate to act until we were 100 percent sure?"

Again, snowflakes could almost be heard crashing onto the ground.

Beneath her dignified exterior, Alice was so angry she wanted to take the ice model and throw it at NoNo.

Louis, the Head Penguin, noticed a change in the group's mood. He said, "If Fred is correct, then we only have the remaining two months until winter begins to react to this threat."

One of the other penguin leaders said, "We need to form a committee from members of this team to analyze the situation and look into possible solutions."

Many of the birds nodded in agreement.

Another one of them told the group, "Yes, but we must do everything possible so that the colony's routines remain intact. Our chicks need a lot of food now to grow, and we need to avoid confusion. So, we *must* keep this a secret until we have worked out a good solution."

Alice cleared her throat loudly, then spoke with a steely resolve. "When we have a problem, forming a committee and trying to protect our colony from unpleasant news is what we normally do. But this is *far, far* from a normal problem."

The others looked at her. The unasked question on everyone's mind was: Where was she going with this line of reasoning?

Alice said, "We must immediately call a general assembly of the colony and convince as many as possible that there is a big problem. We must get enough of our friends and families on our side so that we have a chance of finding a solution that many will accept."

Normally penguins behave in quite a controlled manner, especially if they are Leadership Council penguins sitting in a meeting. But now a few of the birds went completely wild, all talking at the same time.

"An assembly!!" ". . . the risk is . . ." ". . . never have we . . ." ". . . a panic . . ." ". . . no, no, no . . ." ". . . and what would we say?"

It was not a pretty sight.

"I have an idea," Fred said cautiously. "Would you give me a few minutes, please? I won't be long."

The others said nothing. Fred took that to be a yes—or at least not a no.

He moved as quickly as possible down the mountain, found what he wanted, and climbed back up. The Group of Ten birds were jabbering once again. They stopped when Fred arrived with a glass bottle.

"What's this?" asked Alice.

"I don't really know," Fred said. "My father found it one summer washed up to the edge of our iceberg. It looks like ice, but it is not made from ice." He pecked on the bottle with the tip of his beak. "It's much harder than ice and if you sit on it, it warms up but it doesn't melt."

Everyone stared. So . . . ?

"Perhaps we could fill it with water, seal the hole on top, and place it in the cold wind. Then tomorrow we can see if it is broken by the force of the expanding water as it freezes."

Fred paused as the rest of the group worked their way through the logic of his statements.

He continued. "And if it doesn't break apart, then perhaps you should not rush ahead and call an assembly of the colony."

Alice was fascinated. *Risky*, she thought to herself, *but is this bird clever or what?!*

NoNo suspected it was a trick but saw no easy out. And maybe it would stop all the foolishness.

Louis, the Head Penguin, looked at NoNo.

Louis made his judgment. Now was the time to end

this conversation and move on. He told the others, "Then let it be done."

And they did.

Louis put water into the bottle. He sealed it with a fish bone that was just the right size. He gave the bottle to Buddy, a quiet and boyishly handsome penguin who everyone seemed to like and trust.

And then they dispersed.

Fred was always willing to stick his neck out if necessary, though it inevitably made him nervous. So he did not sleep particularly well that night.

The next morning when Buddy climbed up the hill, all the others were there looking down at him. When he reached the top, one of the birds said, "Well?"

Buddy produced the bottle. It was clearly broken from ice that had grown too big to fit inside.

"I'm convinced," Buddy told them.

The birds jabbered for half an hour. All except two said that they needed to act. One of the two, of course, was NoNo. "You may be onto something," he said, "but . . ."

He was more or less ignored.

Louis said, "Let the others know we will have an assembly. Do not tell them the topic yet."

The colony's birds were curious about the reason for the assembly. But Alice made sure the Leadership Council members kept their beaks shut—which built up a bit of interest and suspense.

Nearly all the adults showed up. Most of the talk was about normal life on their iceberg.

"Felix is getting fat. Too much fish, too little exercise."

"Where is he getting all the fish?"

"Ahh, now *that* is an interesting story."

Louis called the meeting to order and quickly turned it over to Alice.

Alice told of her swim with Fred, the many signs

of melting, and the open cave filled with water. Fred showed his model of the iceberg and explained why he thought they were in danger. Buddy told the story of the glass bottle. And Louis, as Head Penguin, watched the group as the others spoke. He could see a clear shift in the crowd. So he ended the session by saying that in his opinion they had to act, and though he was not sure how, he was confident they would find a solution.

By the time everyone had a chance to see the model and the bottle up close, to ask both Fred and Alice questions, and to hear more from Louis, the meeting had lasted most of the morning.

The birds were stunned, even those who normally responded to anything by saying "Well, yes, but . . ." The complacent sense that all is just fine-fine-fine-thank-you began to drain into the vast ocean. Louis ordered the model and bottle to be placed at the center of the community place, where the penguins would frequently come together to work or chat. Instinctively he felt that this would keep the birds from falling back into their normal routines. But he also knew that anxiety could be as harmful as complacency, so he frequently passed the spot to talk to those with worried hearts and minds. Alice saw this, and started to do the same. It was not comfortable for either of them not to have the answers to the horrible problem they faced, but they were encouraged as more and more birds would say something like: "If I can be of help, let me know."

Fred, Louis, and Alice were certainly not aware of it—professional change experts they were not—but by <u>reducing complacency and increasing urgency</u> they had taken exactly the right first step in potentially saving the colony.

I Cannot Do the Job Alone

The next morning a friend of NoNo's slid up to Louis. Penguins can slide on their stomachs, though it looks bizarre to humans. He suggested that as the Head Penguin, it was Louis's *duty* to analyze the problem, make plans, and give out orders for others to execute, thus solving the melting iceberg problem by himself. "That's what leaders do. You are a great leader. You need no help." The bird then slid (one might say slithered) away. Another penguin suggested that Louis delegate the problem to the younger birds who were the experts on ice. Louis pointed out, patiently, that those birds had little credibility in the colony, had no known leadership skills, were very inexperienced, and a few were not well liked. The bird making this suggestion said, "So what's your point?"

Two members of the Group of Ten asked when they would have their first Melting Strategy Session.

Louis thought about what next step he should take, then called Alice, Fred, Buddy, and a penguin named Jordan to a quiet spot on the northwest side of the iceberg. Jordan was known as the "Professor" since he was the closest the Leadership Council had to an intellectual. If a university were located on their iceberg, Jordan would have been a tenured member of the faculty.

The Head Penguin said, "The colony needs a *team* of birds to guide it through this difficult period. I cannot do the job alone. I believe the five of us are the best team for the task ahead."

Alice nodded ever so slightly. Buddy looked confused. Fred was surprised that he, a relatively junior penguin, was being included. But the Professor was the first to speak.

"Why do you make the assumption that the five of us can succeed?" he asked.

Louis nodded in his normal patient manner. Alice hid

her irritation. If she had had a watch, which she didn't, she would have been looking at it while tapping her foot.

"It is a reasonable question," the Head Penguin said. "Look at the five of us, Professor. Define the challenge clearly. Make a list in your mind of each of our strengths. Deduce an answer to your own question."

Louis never talked this way, except when he was speaking to the Professor.

Jordan looked off toward the horizon. If you could have heard the thoughts flashing through his penguin brain, they would have been something like this:

- **Louis:** Head Penguin. Enough experience to be wise. Patient. A bit conservative. Not easily flustered. Respected by almost all except NoNo and the teenagers. Smart (but not an intellectual heavyweight).
- **Alice:** Practical. Aggressive. Makes things happen. Doesn't care about status and treats everyone the same. Impossible to intimidate, so don't even try. Smart (but not an intellectual heavyweight).

- **Buddy:** Boyishly handsome. Not the slightest bit ambitious. Well trusted and liked by almost everyone (maybe your wife likes him too much). *Definitely* not an intellectual heavyweight.
- **Fred:** Younger. Probably more in touch with junior birds. Amazingly curious and creative. Level-headed. Nice beak. Insufficient data to judge his IQ.
- **Me:** Logical (actually, very logical). Well read. Fascinated by interesting questions. Not the most social of birds, but then why would anyone want to be a social bird?
- All of us appear to feel a sense of urgency to act, and *now*. Thus, if the Head Penguin is A, Alice is B, Buddy is C, Fred is D, I am E, and urgency is F, then A + B + C + D + E + F clearly equals a strong group.

The Professor turned to Louis and said, "What you say is remarkably logical."

Buddy looked confused, as he often did. He never

really understood the Professor, but he trusted Louis. Alice's irritation calmed a bit as she was once again reminded of why the Head Penguin was the Head Penguin.

Fred couldn't imagine what went on in the Professor's head. But like Alice and Louis, Fred sensed they were on the right track. He also felt privileged to be asked to work with this talented group of senior birds.

Louis softly told them: "I agree with Jordan. But . . . if anyone feels uncomfortable with the idea of working with us, or is simply too busy now with other responsibilities, you must speak up. I am not ordering this group to be together."

Buddy blinked (actually not looking confused!). You could almost see the Professor's brain doing its calculations. And Alice nodded gently.

"I'm in," she said. After a brief pause, the Professor nodded, then Buddy, and finally Fred.

They spent the rest of the day together. The conversation was difficult at first:

"I wonder by what percentage our home is shrinking

each year," the Professor said at one point. "I once read that a bird named Vladiwitch created a method . . ."

Alice coughed twice. Loudly. While staring intensely at Louis, she said, "Maybe we should concentrate on what we are going to do tomorrow."

Buddy said softly, "I'm sure Mr. Vladiwitch was a very nice bird."

The Professor nodded, pleased that someone was joining his conversation, even if it was only Buddy.

Louis redirected the dialogue. "I think it would help if we all closed our eyes for a moment." Before the Professor could question the relevance of eye closing, the Head Penguin said, "Please don't ask why. Tolerate an old bird's suggestion. This will only require a minute."

The others, one after the other, closed their eyes.

Louis said, "With your eyes shut, point east." After a moment of hesitation, all did so. "Now open your eyes," he told them.

Buddy, the Professor, Fred, and Alice all pointed in different directions. Buddy even pointed slightly upward toward the sky.

Alice sighed, intuitively sensing the problem. The Professor said, "Ah, yes, fascinating." Fred nodded ever so slightly.

The Professor said, "You see, for us, A + B is additive—that is to say, more capable than two individuals by themselves—only if A and B can work as a team, only if they share some desires, ambitions, and perspectives. Yet we responded to Louis's task as individuals, obviously each with a very different sense of where east was. He did not say we couldn't work together, could not talk or touch each other. You see, Flotbottom's theory of group . . ."

The Head Penguin interrupted the speech by raising his wing, then saying "Would anyone like squid for lunch?" This stopped the overweight Professor, whose grumbling stomach easily trumped his brain. Buddy said, "What a great idea."

Penguins *love* squid, those sea creatures that come in sizes ranging from as large as a bus—like Jules Verne's monster in *20,000 Leagues Under the Sea*—to smaller than a mouse. But the tiny squid so liked by the penguins are tricky little devils. They will shoot a very unappealing jet of black ink at a predator and then zoom away. So in a one squid versus one penguin matchup, the squid can easily win. Penguins, having discovered this problem many, many years ago, had found a solution: hunt squid in groups.

Louis jumped into the sea first, quickly followed by the others. Although penguins wobble awkwardly back and forth on land—looking a bit like Charlie Chaplin—in the water they move with extraordinary skill and grace. They can dive a third of a mile beneath the surface, stay underwater for up to twenty minutes, and maneuver better than a $250,000 Porsche. But . . . extraordinary individual capabilities do not a squid catch.

The first squid they encountered actually escaped. But soon the penguins learned to work together well—coordinating their movements, surrounding the lunch. Eventually, enough food for everyone was found, even for the Professor's rather large appetite.

After a satisfying meal, Louis led a discussion that rarely touched on the melting iceberg or what the five of them needed to do next. Instead he focused on life, loved ones, and their hopes and dreams. They talked for hours and, rather oddly under the circumstances, less about problems and hazards and more about aspirations and opportunities.

The Professor was disinclined to just talk about life without structure around the conversation to give it some *rigor*. So he kept his beak shut and let his analytical brain work quietly. Melting iceberg. Fred finds it. Tough sell to a complacent group. Goes to Alice first. Shows her the problem. The ice model. The bottle. The group meeting. Complacency reduced. Louis picks out a potential group to guide the effort. Interesting makeup. Does not appoint. Asks for help. Turning non-team into team with squid and talk. Then somehow end up talking of possibilities and dreams!

All rather strange, but fascinating.

The next morning, Louis asked them to stay together. He would have liked a month to turn the five birds into a close-knit team. But he did not have a month. So he did the best he could, and within two days the penguins certainly looked much less like individuals pointing in different directions. Louis had largely succeeded in taking the difficult but essential step of <u>pulling together a team to guide the needed change</u>.

The Seagull

An impatient Alice suggested they search rapidly for solutions to their melting-iceberg problem by talking to others in the colony. "We need more brains helping us." The Head Penguin was not sure that talking to others was the best next step, and the Professor definitely did not see the point. "What brains?!" But after a constructive discussion, Alice prevailed.

One bird—who had the heart of a Texas oilman—suggested they drill a hole from the surface down to the cave to let out water and pressure. This would not solve the more general problem of the melting, but it might keep their home from exploding during the upcoming winter. This drill-a-hole idea was briefly discussed before the Professor pointed out that with all 268 birds pecking away 24 hours a day, they would break through to the cave in 5.2 years.

Another bird suggested they find a perfect iceberg. No melting, no exposed caves, no fissures, just wonderful in every way so that their children and grandchildren would never, ever have to face a crisis like this again. Perhaps if they appointed a perfect-iceberg committee? Fortunately, Alice was not around to hear this.

Another idea: somehow move the colony toward the center of Antarctica where the ice is thicker and stronger. Although none of the penguins had any idea of the size of the continent—more than one and a half times the size of the United States!—one very heavyset bird said, "Won't that take us a long way from water? How will I get food?"

One penguin on the Leadership Council suggested creating a sort of superglue out of killer-whale blubber and using it to glue the iceberg together "real tight." He admitted that this would not solve the more general problem of melting, but it might avert immediate disaster.

They were obviously getting desperate.

Then an older and highly respected member of the colony suggested that they try something new. "Maybe you should do what Fred did when he found our terrible problem. Walk around, keeping your eyes and minds open. Be curious." The Head Penguin, recognizing the need for a different approach, agreed. "Let's try it," he said, and so they did.

They went west. They saw beautiful walls of snow. They saw families doing things families do. They overheard conversations about melting and fish. They listened to birds who needed to share their anxieties.

Then after an hour or so, Fred, in his typically respectful way, said: "Up there."

Fred was looking at a seagull. Since normally there are no seagulls in Antarctica, they all stared. A small, white, flying penguin? Probably not.

"Fascinating," said the Professor. "I have a theory about animals that fly. You see—" Before he could continue, Alice tapped him on his shoulder. He had learned in the prior two days that Alice tapping him like that meant "You're wonderful, Professor, but please shut up," which he did.

"What is it?" asked Buddy.

"I don't know," Fred said, "but a bird can't fly forever. It must have a home on the ground. But it's so cold here."

They agreed. If the seagull tried to live with them, it would freeze as hard as a rock in less than a week.

Fred continued, "I suppose it could be very, very lost, but it does not seem to be afraid. What if moving from one piece of land to another was just the way it lived? What if it's a . . ."

Fred used the closest word penguins have for "nomad."

Alice said, "You aren't suggesting . . . ?"

The Head Penguin said, "I wonder."

The Professor said, "Fascinating."

Buddy said, "I'm sorry, but what are you talking about?"

The Head Penguin responded to Buddy by saying, simply, "We are thinking about the possibility of a new and very different way of life."

They talked for hours and hours. If we . . . But then . . . How would we . . . ? No, you see . . . Yes, but we could . . . Why not . . . ? Just maybe . . .

Buddy asked, "So what do we do next?"

The Head Penguin said, "We need to think this through carefully."

Alice said, "We need to move fast."

The Professor said, "But quality of thought is more important than speed."

Alice continued, "Whatever! But first we need to learn more about that flying bird, and now."

The Head Penguin agreed. The Professor went looking for something to write on. Then they all went to search for the seagull.

Fred had in him a bit of Sherlock Holmes, the

famous non-penguin detective. So within a half hour, they found the seagull.

Alice whispered to Buddy, "Say 'hello' to the bird."

In the warm and gentle voice that came naturally, Buddy said, "Hi. This is Alice." He pointed at her. "That's Louis, Fred, and the Professor. I'm Buddy."

The seagull just stared at them.

"Where do you come from?" Buddy asked. "And what are you looking for here?"

The seagull kept its distance, but did not fly away. Finally he said, "I'm a scout. I fly ahead of the clan looking for where we might live next."

The Professor began to ask questions—useful questions, though he did go off on tangents occasionally (always brought back by You-Know-Who).

In response, the seagull told the penguins of his clan's nomadic existence. He talked about what they ate (which, frankly, sounded to the penguins like just about anything). He spoke of what it was like to be a scout. When he began to turn blue and have trouble speaking, he said good-bye and flew away.

The Professor and Buddy were not totally convinced that what was appropriate for seagulls could possibly be right for penguins. "We're different." "They fly." "We eat delicious fresh fish." "They seem to eat, well . . . yuck."

"Of course we're different," Alice said with considerably more diplomacy than usual. "That means we can't just copy them. But the idea is very interesting. I can almost see how we might live. We'd learn to move around. We wouldn't stay in one place forever. We wouldn't try to fix melting icebergs. We would just face up to the fact that what sustains us cannot go on forever."

The Professor asked dozens of questions. Louis said little but thought a great deal about the discussion and its implications.

Alice said, "I wonder why someone didn't think of this idea as soon as we realized that our iceberg was melting."

The Professor said, "Surely *someone* in the colony did. It is so . . . logical."

The Professor turned his head to the right. What he saw was:

Well, the Professor thought, *maybe not*.

The Head Penguin said, "After living one way for so long, why should it be easy to think of a whole new way of life?"

The Professor realized that no one had offered a solid theory about why their home was melting. He had been assuming that melting and degradation must have occurred slowly over a long period of time. But what if that weren't true?

What if something had caused the problem suddenly? But what could that possibly be? Should he have urged his fellow penguins to take more time and be more systematic in thinking about their iceberg problem? But there was so little time.

Unanswered questions disturbed the Professor greatly. But that evening, he slept remarkably well under the circumstances. He believed the team had succeeded in creating a vision of a new future, and one that seemed plausible. He was beginning to see how they could create that future. He was (oddly) comforted that Louis, Alice, Fred, and Buddy were thinking the same way.

Getting the Message Out

The following day, Louis called for a meeting at noon of the entire colony. As you would expect at this point, nearly everyone showed up—so there would be again no lunch for the increasingly desperate leopard seals.

An energized Professor spent the entire morning preparing a sort of 97-slide PowerPoint presentation for Louis to use in communicating their vision. The Head Penguin looked over the material, which was very impressive, then gave it to Buddy. After studying the Professor's work, Buddy said, "I'm sorry, but I'm a little lost." Louis asked where he had become stuck. Buddy told him it was on slide #2. Alice shut her eyes and did deep breathing exercises.

The Head Penguin looked again at the presentation created by the Professor. It was, in its way, beautifully done. But Louis kept thinking about how difficult it would be to help the colony understand his message. How do you talk to those birds who were anxious, preoccupied, skeptical, tradition bound, or unimaginative?

Louis decided he needed to try a different method, even though it could be risky. He did not like risk, but . . .

Louis began the colony's assembly by saying, "Fellow penguins, as we meet this challenge—*and we definitely will*—it is more important than ever to remember *who we really are.*"

The crowd looked blankly at him.

"Tell me, are we penguins who deeply respect one another?"

There was silence until someone said, "Of course." Then others said, "Yes."

NoNo was in the middle of the audience trying to figure out what scheme was afoot. It was not obvious yet, which he did not like.

Louis continued. "And do we strongly value discipline?" "Yes," said a dozen or so of the elderly birds.

"And do we have a strong sense of responsibility, too?" It was hard to argue with that. It had been true for generations.

"Yes," many now agreed.

"Above all, do we stand for brotherhood and the love of our young?"

A loud "Yes!" followed.

The Head Penguin paused. "And tell me . . . are these qualities that say who we are and what we care about linked to *a large piece of ice*?"

When some not particularly bright birds, caught up in the yes-yes cadence, were again about to say yes, Alice shouted, "NO!" She was quickly followed by the Professor, Fred, and a few of the younger birds. Then many penguins muttered a "No, no, no" to themselves.

"No," Louis agreed.

The birds stood still, all looking at the Head Penguin. Some didn't know that he could speak so forcefully—and so emotionally.

"I'd like you now to listen to Buddy," Louis said after another dramatic pause. "He will tell you a story that inspired us to think of a new and better way of life."

So Buddy started to tell the seagull's story: "He is a scout for his clan. He explores the territory to find good places for his colony to move next. *Imagine, they are free! They go wherever they like to go.* You see, many, many years ago, they . . ."

Buddy told what he knew of the history of the seagull clan, of the way they lived now, and of the bird he had met. Buddy wasn't aware of it, but he was a very good storyteller.

When he was done, the penguins had many questions. Some of the slower birds struggled with the idea of a flying animal. Some just wanted to know every detail of what the seagull had said. There were many side discussions, especially about "freedom" and a nomadic existence. The faster birds were quick to see the vision without it ever being stated explicitly.

Louis let the jabbering go on for a while. Then he cleared his throat loudly and asked for order. When the noise subsided, he told the crowd, with conviction, "This iceberg is not who we *are*. It is only where we now *live*. We are smarter, stronger, and more capable than the seagulls. So why can't we do what they have done, and better? We are not chained to this piece of ice. We can leave it behind us. Let it melt to the size of a fish. Let it break into one thousand pieces. We will find other places to live that are safer . . . and better! When necessary, we will move again. We will never have to put our families at risk from the sort of terrible danger we face today. *We will prevail!*"

NoNo's blood pressure hit 240 over 160.

By the end of the meeting, if you could have carefully studied the eyes of the crowd, you would probably have concluded that:

- 30 percent of the colony could see a new way of living, were convinced the vision had merit, and were relieved. As many as a third of them, a full 10 percent of the colony, looked as if they would volunteer on the spot to do about anything to make this happen.
- 30 percent were digesting what they had heard and seen;
- 20 percent were very confused;
- 10 percent were skeptical but not hostile; and
- 10 percent were like NoNo, convinced this was all completely absurd.

The Head Penguin thought to himself, *Good enough for now*, and so he ended the meeting.

Alice grabbed Fred, Buddy, and the Professor, and said, "Follow me." Being sensible birds, they did so.

She quickly explained her latest idea: to come up with slogans to be put on ice-posters. "We need to remind the birds of what they have heard, and remind them *all the time*. The meeting this morning was brief. Some of the colony were not here. The message is radical. We need much more communication—every day, everywhere."

Buddy wondered aloud, "Will so many posters be annoying to some of our friends?" Alice replied, "Given a choice between a few annoyed birds and a melting, exploding iceberg with screaming penguins on it, I'd choose annoyed." Put that way . . .

They began creating posters. At first they struggled.

But with the help of some of the more creative birds—some of whom were younger than Fred and virtually all of whom did not have to be convinced to assist the effort once they heard of it—they quickly got the hang of it.

Every day for a week, at least twenty penguins came up with new slogans and put them on ice-posters scattered around the iceberg. When the birds could find no more places for the posters, someone suggested they put them underwater next to the most popular and productive fishing grounds. Sounds a little odd, but (1) penguins can see very clearly underwater, (2) there were no posters there yet, and (3) when penguins look for fish, they cannot close their eyes, even if they are annoyed.

Buddy reached out to some of his friends and they created "talking circles" where Louis, Alice, or Fred would start the conversation and then the whole group would speak about a nomadic life. "I can take a group or two," the Professor announced. Buddy was too embarrassed to say this might not be such a great idea, so he was relieved when Alice stepped in and said, "Jordan, you are amazing at lecturing but that is not exactly what we need here. We need to let the birds talk. Think about it." Which he did, and although a tiny bit hurt he admitted after a second or two, "That's logical."

The dramatic meeting, Louis's "we are not an iceberg" speech, Buddy's storytelling about the seagull, the countless ice-posters, and the talking circles began to have the desired effect. Many birds, though hardly all, came to see and accept what they had to do. Complacency, fear, and confusion continued to decrease. What had started out with a threat had turned, at least in a number of bird heads and hearts, into an opportunity. Optimism and excitement grew.

Communicating the new vision of a nomadic life, of a very different future, was for the most part remarkably successful.

The colony had taken yet another big step forward. You could tell just by watching the birds.

Good News, Bad News

Thirty to forty birds began to work in small groups to plan for the selection of scouts, the mapping of trips to find new icebergs, and the logistics of moving the colony. Louis was cautiously optimistic, not least because so many of the birds were actively, enthusiastically helping with the work.

Over the next week, there was both good news and bad.

Good: Although some birds were still anxious, an optimistic energy among the core group of planners continued to grow and grow.

Mostly Good: Nearly two dozen birds expressed interest in being scouts—the job of looking for a new home for the colony. Unfortunately, at least at first, the group was mostly made up of adolescents who showed less concern for finding a new iceberg than for putting more excitement into lives that lacked video games and Nikes.

Not So Good: NoNo and a few of his friends seemed to be everywhere forecasting storms and dangerous currents. Many penguins ignored them, but far from all. Some mid-level birds, with much of the responsibility of making the colony function on a daily basis, often at least listened when NoNo screamed, "This nonsense is creating chaos!"

Mysterious: A few of the very young penguins started having scary dreams. When Alice looked into the problem, she found that the kindergarten teacher had developed an affinity for telling the children horror stories about ghastly killer whales hunting young penguins. The nightmares caused much uproar among the parents, including some who had volunteered to become scouts. Why was the good-natured teacher creating this problem?

Not Mysterious at All, but Certainly Not Helpful: Some members of the Leadership Council thought the scouts would need a boss. When they began to lobby for the role of Head of the Scouts, irritating conflict among the Council members grew.

And finally, there was . . .

Very Troubling News: Penguins need a lot of food to build up fat for the winter. Someone pointed out that the difficult task of exploring the vast territory around the iceberg would leave the scouts with insufficient time to fish. This problem was made much worse because of a long-standing tradition in the colony that birds shared their food with their children, and *only* with their children. No adults caught fish for other adults. It simply was not done.

The effect of the good news at first outweighed the bad. But then NoNo's antics, anxious children, anxiety among the parents of anxious children, infighting in the Leadership Council, the raised eyebrows of some mid-level penguins, and the feeding-the-scouts problem began to take their toll.

NoNo and a few of his friends saw the obstacles and were encouraged. Maybe if they worked a little harder . . .

✳ ✳ ✳

Amanda was one of the most enthusiastic and hardworking of the birds in the group of planners. She believed in the vision of a new way of life. She worked fourteen-hour days to help make it a reality. But then her husband, unnerved by NoNo's pronouncements, demanded that she stop. Long, difficult conversations ensued. Then her child's nightmares became so chilling that she found herself spending half the night tending to the little bird. When she heard about the feeding-the-scouts problem, her level of frustration outgrew her initial excitement. Feeling powerless to deal with forces beyond her control, she started to skip the planning meetings.

And she was not alone.

By Thursday that week, three other birds were also missing the meetings. By Friday, that number had grown to eight; by Saturday, to fifteen.

The bird that was most helpful facilitating those meetings tried to stop the outflow of membership with a clear restatement of the facts. *Iceberg melting. Must change. Have a good vision. Time for implementation.* The logic was impeccable. And it had almost no effect on the dropping attendance.

Alice saw that many of the more enthusiastic birds were becoming very frustrated by the mounting obstacles. "We have to deal with this," she told Louis, "and quickly." He agreed.

Buddy, Fred, the Professor, Louis, and Alice discussed the situation, identified what needed to be done, and agreed upon what role each of them would play. Such quick agreement was not necessarily a sign of panic, but close to it.

Even as they met, NoNo was everywhere.

"The gods are very mad," he told crowd after crowd. "They will send a gigantic killer whale to eat all our fish. Its enormous mouth will bite our iceberg into pieces and crush our children in its awful jaws. It will create five-hundred-foot waves. We must stop this nonsense about 'nomads' *immediately.*"

Louis pulled NoNo aside and told him (truthfully) that weather forecasting would be more important in the future and that they needed to add more science to their approach.

NoNo listened, warily.

"Therefore," Louis said, "I have asked the Professor to help us."

NoNo angrily turned around to leave and found the Professor was already beside him.

"Did you read the article by Himlish on iceberg trauma?" the Professor asked. "I believe it was published in the late 1960s." NoNo ran. The Professor followed.

And *everywhere* that NoNo went . . .

In a very direct way, Louis also dealt with those lobbying to be Head of the Scouts.

It was a short, very firm discussion. "Enough!" he told them.

Alice wanted to hit some mid-level penguins on their heads for acting like NoNo and putting up barriers to those who were helping. But after some thought, she followed a different route, hesitating at first. At the next regular meeting of mid-level birds, and after some initial words about the stakes involved if they did not move quickly into a new and different future, she called three of them to stand next to her. She explained to all that she had been told that these three were being very helpful in supporting the extra work being put in by some of the excited birds to deal with the problem of melting. She shook the fins of all three, thanked them, and gave words of praise. The meeting no doubt had zero effect on NoNo's hard-core allies, but it clearly made most in the crowd stop and think.

Buddy explained to Louis, Fred, Alice, and the Professor that he wanted to talk to the kindergarten teacher. They immediately liked his idea—including the Professor, who was baffled at how Buddy could possibly think of such a clever scheme.

So the bird nearly everyone liked sought out the

teacher. Without hesitation she shared her fears—fears that clearly had been influencing her choice of the stories she was reading to the children.

"With all the change," she told him, nearly sobbing, "the colony may not need a kindergarten. It, it . . . may not need a teacher who is a bit too old to adapt."

She was very upset. Buddy was very sympathetic. When she stopped speaking, he told her: "No. The little birds will need to learn even *more* in a world that will be ever changing. A kindergarten will be *more* important."

Her sobbing slowed. Buddy continued to speak of the essential role of schooling after all the changes.

"I am very confident," he concluded, with complete sincerity, "that you can help them learn what is needed. You are a wonderful teacher. If you need to make adjustments here and there, I know you'll do it because you care so much for the little ones."

He was reassuring. He was patient. He calmly and sincerely repeated his message again and again. She felt so relieved and happy that she wanted to kiss him.

It was a truly touching scene.

The actions by Louis, Alice, the Professor, and Buddy—with still others by Fred—all had an immediate effect.

NoNo created no new mischief (though he certainly wanted to). No matter where he went, the Professor was right beside him, talking and talking and talking.

"A regression of six variables has shown . . ."

"If you don't stop following me," NoNo screamed, "I'm going to . . ."

"Yes, yes. Now pay particular attention to this point. The regression . . ."

"Aaaggggh . . ."

After her chat with Buddy, the kindergarten teacher gathered her young students together to tell them tales of heroic action to help others under difficult and changing circumstances. She found some great stories. She told them with enthusiasm.

She explained that the colony would be needing heroes to deal with new challenges, and that anyone, including the youngest of them, could help. The students loved it.

That same evening, most of the nightmares stopped.

The number of penguins actively working in the core group had dropped from thirty-five to eighteen. But now, as obstacles to change were being removed, as fewer and fewer of the more enthusiastic birds were feeling frustrated, distracted, or powerless, the numbers began to rise again.

Louis calculated that they would need at least fifty birds to do all the work that had to be completed quickly. He didn't have fifty yet, but at least the trend was again heading in the right direction.

Sally Ann was just a kindergarten student. Her mind was filled with all the new stories of heroic action. While waddling home from school, she saw Alice. As youngsters do when they don't know any better, she approached this important bird and said, "Excuse me. How can I become a hero?" Alice stopped and looked at her. Preoccupied with the melting, the general mood of the colony, and the feeding-the-scouts problem, she barely heard the question. The youngster repeated it. Instead of saying, "Just go home to your mother," Alice told her, "If you could make your parents understand that the Head Penguin needs their help, especially in catching fish to feed the scouts, then you would be a true hero."

"That's all?" the little one replied, with all the hopeful naiveté of the young.

The next day, the child talked to her friends, and she had many friends. And from those discussions, an idea was born of how the children could help the colony make a nomadic life a reality. The kindergarten teacher canceled a few regular classes—broke a few rules—and helped give the idea some structure. It came to be called "Tribute to Our Heroes Day."

Some parents were nervous about all this activity. Knocking down barriers to <u>making everyone</u>, even the children, <u>feel empowered</u> was unprecedented in the colony. But the chicks loved it.

The Scouts

Louis decided they would need more evidence, and quickly, that their efforts were on the right track. So his next step was to ask Fred to select a small, elite group of athletic and highly motivated birds, who would be willing to be the first wave of scouts, out searching for potential new homes.

"The colony needs to see more progress as soon as possible," the Head Penguin told Fred. "And we must do everything conceivable to help the scouts devise the means to protect themselves. We need every one of those birds to return safely and as fast as possible. Even one missing bird will create anxiety and make NoNo's warnings more credible. Remember, they don't need to pick a new home, just find us a few possibilities."

Fred chose a strong, bright, and highly enthusiastic

group of scouts from an even larger group who professed they were more than willing to take on the task. Given the uncertainties and dangers involved, all the volunteering was almost hard to believe.

The toughest single challenge facing the colony was gathering enough fresh fish to feed the tired and hungry scouts when they returned to their home. They would each need a huge meal of fish immediately—up to twenty pounds worth which, incredibly, a penguin can easily eat at one sitting.

But . . . there was that very old tradition in the colony in which birds (1) shared their food with their children, and (2) shared their food *only* with their children.

So who would catch fish for the scouts?

Into the void of practical solutions came little Sally Ann, the kindergartner, with her "Tribute to Our Heroes Day" idea.

The Heroes Day celebration would include a raffle, performances, a band, and a flea market. The unusual price of admission: two fish per adult.

The young birds explained the festive day to their parents. As you might imagine, some preoccupied adults could not quite grasp what they were hearing, some did not like the idea much at all, and some were not even aware that scouts had left the iceberg. Yet many were proud of their children for being creative in a time of need.

Still, parents felt a bit awkward. "You don't share food, except with your children" was a very, very old and established tradition. So the inspired youngsters made it clear that they would be *extremely* embarrassed unless (1) their parents came to Heroes Day, and (2) each mother and father brought two fish as the cost of admission.

As soon as a few parents relented, announcing that they would be bringing fish, others decided they must also. Social pressure works as well in penguin colonies as in human colonies.

Louis scheduled Heroes Day to coincide with the time the scouts were scheduled to return. From early in the morning until late in the afternoon, the event was an astonishing success. The games, band, raffle, and other events were great fun for everyone. But the climax came at the end, as the birds waited for the scouts.

NoNo predicted half would never make it back. "Whale food," he told as many as would listen to him. "The fools will get lost." Some birds nodded their heads, so he kept saying it. NoNo worked harder that day than he had in years.

Some in the colony were nervous, quite apart from NoNo's antics. Some were still skeptical about the claims being made. All of which made the end of the day even more dramatic.

Every single scout returned, one after the other, although a few looked like they were at death's door, and one was seriously hurt. Alice was waiting with a well-organized crew to care for any injury. Which they did.

Almost as soon as the scouts arrived, they began to tell amazing tales about the sea, about swimming long distances, and about new icebergs they had seen. Everyone crowded around the birds.

Because they were so hungry, the scouts quickly and happily ate the fish that the other penguins had brought to the fair. Even as they were stuffing themselves, you could see that most of Fred's volunteers were extremely excited about what they had done. When they were finished, Sally Ann and her little friends gave the scouts ribbons to go around their necks. Made by the children, the ribbons were all tied to glittering ice medals with the simple inscription, HERO.

The crowd cheered. The scouts beamed (or at least as much as penguins can beam).

Louis called for the child who had put in motion the events leading to the festive day. In front of the colony, he said, "And this is for our youngest hero." He handed Sally Ann the broken bottle, which had become somewhat legendary since first shown to all the birds. The crowd applauded enthusiastically.

The child cried small tears of joy. Her parents were puffed up with pride. Alice was as happy as she could remember being in years.

Discussions went late into the night, well after the children had been put to bed. Many in the colony continued to be amazed at what the scouts told them, even when it was said a second or third time. Most of the birds who were skeptical of a nomadic life found themselves becoming much less skeptical. Birds who were enthusiastic felt more enthusiastic. Again, under trying circumstances, the colony had taken a very important step forward.

Fred and the scouts had succeeded in creating (what one MBA-sounding bird called) "a short-term win." And it was a big win.

NoNo was nowhere in sight. He seemed to have been magically replaced by scouts wearing ribbons attached to medals.

The Second Wave

The next morning, Louis called a meeting of the scouts. The Professor was also invited.

"What did you learn?" the Head Penguin asked the birds. "What icebergs did you see that might be big enough, in good shape, able to protect our eggs during the winter, and close enough so that our children and elderly can safely travel there?"

The scouts discussed what they had found. The Professor asked question after question after question to distinguish opinions from facts. His style did not make him popular with all the birds—he could not have cared less—but it was very effective.

After the Heroes Day, even more birds volunteered to be among the second wave of scouts, though their task of selecting a single iceberg might be very taxing. Louis chose a team from among the volunteers and sent them off to explore promising possibilities discovered by the first wave of scouts.

Many of the skeptics in the colony were now becoming much less skeptical. Some birds still had reservations, many of which were rational. A few of the penguins were just nervous by nature.

Almost no one was paying any attention to NoNo anymore.

Alice was relentless in keeping up the momentum of the work. Some on the Leadership Council complained that they did not have time to deal with all the issues that were arising. Alice pointed out that half their traditional Leadership Council meetings were irrelevant. "Eliminate them," she said bluntly. Louis did.

At one point, even the Head Penguin suggested that the right step might be to slow down. But Alice wouldn't hear of it.

"We are constantly at risk of losing our courage. Some birds are already suggesting we wait until next winter. Then, if we are still alive, they will say the danger was overstated and that any change is not needed."

It was a good point.

The second wave of scouts found an iceberg that looked suitable for a number of reasons. It was:

- A safe home. No evidence of melting or water-filled caves.
- Equipped with a tall snow wall to protect them from the icy storms.
- Close to good fishing sites.
- Located on a route with enough small icebergs or ice plateaus along the way to give the youngest and oldest penguins some rest during the journey.

The returning scouts were proud, excited, and very happy. The rest of the colony was proud, excited, and happy to see them.

By this time, the chore of gathering fish for scouts was already beginning to seem like a part of the normal routine. Many birds helped. It was all rather astonishing.

The Professor was asked to assess more scientifically the newly found piece of ice and snow. He was not very enthusiastic about this task. He was overweight and the journey to the new iceberg was not a short one. But after a quiet chat with Louis (and a not so quiet chat with Alice), he announced he was ready to accompany a group of scouts. And he did.

Meanwhile, the colony was busy with other important, though pleasant, routines, like creating new little penguins.

Then on May 12, just before the start of Antarctica's winter, the birds began their move to their new home. It was not a moment too soon.

The move was chaotic at times. At one point, a few penguins were lost and there was a panic. But those birds found their way back to the others, and for the most part, all went as well as one could hope.

Because of his effective leadership, Louis became greatly admired by the colony. Yet, to his credit, he did not allow his pride to slide into arrogance.

Buddy soothed the worried, encouraged the downtrodden, calmed the frantic, and probably had another ten female birds fall in love with him (but that's another story).

When no one could think of a solution to a new problem, Fred was called in to display his level-headed creativity.

The Professor loved his new status in the colony. He even found, oddly, that he enjoyed the admiration of birds he thought had no brains at all.

Alice seemed to exist on three hours of sleep a day.

And NoNo predicted doom until the very end.

The winter passed. The colony had problems. Their new home was different, the best fishing grounds were in unfamiliar places, the winds bounced off walls of ice in unexpected ways. But the problems were not as large as the most anxious birds had feared.

The next season, the scouts found a still better iceberg, larger and with richer fishing grounds. And though it was tempting to declare that the colony had been subjected to enough change, and should stay forever on their new home, they didn't. They moved again. It was a critical step: not becoming complacent again and <u>not letting up</u>.

As you might imagine, the preparation for the second move was much less traumatic than the first.

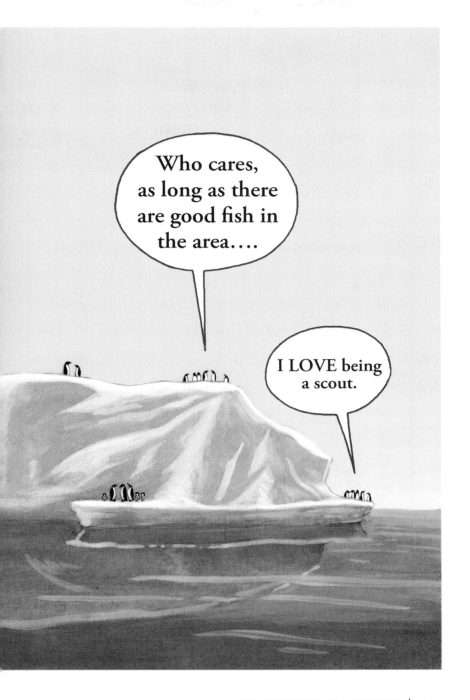

The Most Remarkable Change

You might reasonably think our story is over. But it isn't quite.

Some birds began to talk about how they had now found the perfect iceberg and therefore . . .

Tradition dies a hard death. Culture changes with as much difficulty in penguin colonies as in human colonies. But with this colony, culture did change. And in a number of ways.

Louis, Buddy, Fred, Alice, and the Professor continued to have discussions. The Sally Anns of the colony, some of the birds that had helped Alice with the ice-posters, any number of the scouts, and more decided they rather liked what they had done and didn't want to stop doing *it*. They didn't have a good penguin word to describe what "it" was. We might use management-speak and say being "change agents." There is a better word (more on that soon). And with some hesitation, Louis didn't stop them from doing *it*.

In one of their talks, Alice (backed up with the Professor's relentless logic) convinced Louis to shake up the Leadership Council. He was reluctant to do anything that would show disrespect for birds who had worked hard for years to help and serve the colony. Making the moves while preserving the dignity of all was not easy. But Alice was insistent, and when Alice was insistent, well, you know.

One of the former scouts was relentless in arguing that they needed a tough selection for scouts, which was required now that so many birds wanted to be scouts! He and the Professor and Fred and another bird (Felix by name) came up with a selection criteria, and Alice and Louis liked it. Another idea some group developed: scouts would be given more fish, less because they needed it—you don't want fat, slow, huffing and puffing scouts—and more as a sign of sincere recognition for what they did.

The Professor insisted that the penguin school system add "scouting" and a number of new subjects to the curriculum. Four birds, including the kindergarten teacher, eagerly volunteered to put together proposals.

Alice and others wanted the Professor to take over as chief weather forecaster. A bit reluctant at first, he eventually volunteered to take on the work, poured "real science" into the task, and came to love the job.

Two of the most respected scouts argued (actually more like jabbered and jabbered and . . .) that Fred serve on the Leadership Council as Head of the Scouts. Alice and Louis both thought that was a great idea. Fred was honored and accepted.

Buddy was offered a number of more important jobs. He turned them all down, but helped the Leadership Council find other good candidates. His lack of ambition came to be seen as great humility. The birds loved him even more.

Louis retired, became the grandfather figure for the whole colony, and enjoyed his free time more than he expected. A now slightly more balanced Alice took his place as Head Penguin.

As time went on, the colony thrived. It grew and grew. It became more skilled at handling new dangers and grabbing new opportunities, at least in part from what it had learned about how to live from the melting adventure.

Sally Ann and a group of her mother's friends met occasionally to talk about never allowing complacency to build again into penguin hearts and minds. They had come to view complacency as quite deadly when you live as nomads in a not so friendly world. They didn't even ask Alice for permission, which a few of them thought was just not right. But they did it anyway.

There was always some tension between those who thought their role was to keep things in order and those who were urgent about producing necessary changes. But most penguins intuitively understood that you needed both to thrive in this new era. Alice would make time in her busy calendar for those who showed promise to become masters in both and also, though somewhat less pleasant, for those who were, let's say, a bit slower.

Grandfather Louis became the colony's number one teacher. He was asked again and again by the younger birds to tell them the story of the First Great Change. He was initially reluctant, fearing that he would sound like an old-timer boasting about past successes—real or imagined. But eventually, he saw the importance of telling the chicks more about the specific steps the colony had taken, and were taking, to cope with change and the various acts of leadership by many that had helped the colony move forward.

Although Louis never said so explicitly, he felt the most remarkable change of all was in how so many members of the colony had grown less afraid of change. The army of volunteers was now an irresistible force of change. And none of those powerful penguins would ever want to miss again the excitement and the learning that happens to all of us when you come together with others to make something extraordinary happen.

The former Head Penguin was particularly amazed at what even the youngsters were already doing to help the colony. And for that, he loved them all the more.

The End

(of the story, not the book)

❄ ❄ ❄

Changing and Succeeding

We hope you have enjoyed our book. If you are the type of person whose mind is already going 100 miles an hour with ideas of what you might do in your very real world, based on insights you have drawn from the story, we would suggest you might just stop here and start doing. Trust your instincts. Make life at work and home better!

If you would like a few other ideas of how you might use the story, we humbly offer them now.

The Penguins and You

The main actors in our tale have much in common with people around us and chances are, with you. So, first, you might think about which bird in the story behaves most like you. Are you a Fred? An Alice? A Louis? A Buddy? A Professor? An enthusiastic volunteer like Sally Ann? Or a combination of two birds? Mostly a Fred, but with some strong Louis lurking in the background?

Whenever you are pursuing new and bold ideas, chances are high that there will be NoNos standing in your way and testing your courage and commitment. Our story's heroes contribute in different ways to the success of the colony. None of them is perfect. All of them are needed. So, you might ask yourself: What other bird or birds do you need most to complement your own talents and, let's say, limitations? This contemplation can be an interesting exercise.

The Eight-Step Process of Successful Change

More and more people are encountering their own melting icebergs. This creates hazards and opportunities at a rate that knows just one direction: up and up. Melting icebergs come in dozens of forms: product lines that are aging, schools that are becoming irrelevant, services that are decreasing in quality, a business strategy that makes increasingly little sense. And quite often we may feel overwhelmed or unprepared to cope with all its consequences. The specific way in which our friends from Antarctica solved their problem and turned it into an opportunity is in fact what we find among the most successful and innovative organizations today, whether they have 100 people or 100,000 people, are privately owned or public, or are high tech or low tech.

We offer you the following summary to help you lead

change. It shows the Eight Steps to successfully implement change, and asks you to think about these in relation to your situation. Who are the Freds that see the opportunities and threats—your iceberg—facing your group, and want to proactively confront them? Is there an Alice who helps their voices be heard? How did our bird friends accomplish step one? Step two? Steps six and eight? Then take it into your world. Where are you in your change or strategy implementation process? Where have you made progress? What are some of the barriers that slow you down? On which step or steps do you need to direct your energy and attention now? Honestly assessing your situation and thinking about these questions periodically never fails to be helpful.

SET THE STAGE

1. Create a Sense of Urgency.

Help others see the need for change and the importance of acting immediately. Develop more and more energy dedicated to action.

Consider: Do we have a strong "why" for our change? Are enough people convinced that we must do something about it? What is our iceberg model, or bottle, to help others see and feel the need for change?

2. Pull Together the Guiding Team.

Make sure there is a powerful group guiding the change—one with leadership skills, credibility, communications ability, authority, analytical skills, and a sense of urgency.

Consider: Do we have a core group of penguins who share that sense of urgency, like Louis, Alice, Buddy, Fred, and the Professor? Are they working well together as a team or do they need to go for a squid hunt?

DECIDE WHAT TO DO

3. Develop the Change Vision and Strategy.

Clarify how the future will be different from the past, and how you can make that future a reality.

Consider: What would be the equivalent of becoming nomads and being "free"? Is that better future attractive enough? Do we have a credible path to achieve that goal? Is there a guide like the seagull, or a role model to learn from?

MAKE IT HAPPEN

4. Communicate for Understanding and Buy-In.

Make sure as many others as possible understand and accept the vision and the strategy. Go beyond "stopping resistance" to creating more and more people who want to help you.

Consider: Do we have communication tactics like ice-posters and talking circles? Are there enough participants from every rank of the organization helping us communicate the message?

5. Empower Others to Act.

Remove as many barriers as possible so that those who want to make the vision a reality can do so. Encourage others to remove barriers and make true innovation happen.

Consider: Who are the planners and scouts who believe in the vision and want to help make it a reality? Have we made it clear where we want and need their help? Do we have enough? Is there a plan to deal with the NoNos, crying kindergarteners, and other barriers to success?

6. Produce Short-Term Wins.

Create some visible, unambiguous successes as soon as possible—something that makes today better than yesterday and tomorrow better than today. Whenever feasible, communicate and celebrate these "wins."

Consider: Have we given the scouts a first goal that they can reach fast enough to win over the skeptics? Can we organize something like a Heroes Day to recognize the contributions of our heroes and celebrate progress?

7. Don't Let Up.

Press harder and faster after the first successes. Be relentless with initiating change after change until the vision is a reality.

Consider: Have we raised the bar for the next wave of scouts? Which meetings are no longer needed and can be canceled, so we don't exhaust ourselves? What else can we do to keep the momentum going?

MAKE IT STICK

8. Create a New Culture.

Hold on to the new ways of behaving, and make sure they succeed, until they become strong enough to replace old traditions. Better still, make all of these steps a central part of the way you live to help you adapt to an ever faster changing world.

Consider: Are we putting those who have helped make change happen in leadership roles? Have the scouts been rewarded? How can we institutionalize change, like adding scouting to the school curriculum?

The Power of Group Discussions

Finally, consider the power of group discussion. Far too few teams going through change have a shared mental map or even a shared language of the predictable challenges they are facing and smart ways of dealing with those issues. The word "alignment" is used a lot these days, and it starts here. So pass the book around to a group of your colleagues. Then set up a time to talk about it. Or add that discussion onto an upcoming meeting that is already scheduled.

Here are a few examples of dialogue from the many helpful meetings of this sort that we have seen over the past decade. Each slice of dialogue was only a few minutes in reality and our attempts to remember the details are far from perfect. The idea here is only to give you a sense of what is possible and encourage you to think about how to lead a conversation that might be helpful for your situation and your team.

Case 1: Icebergs sometimes melt very slowly.

In this first case, around a dozen people met in a room for an hour and a half. The assignment before the session was to read the book and reflect on change efforts in their organization from the recent past—the goal being to learn more from their own experiences and from the experiences of those around them. A piece of the conversation, early in this meeting, went something like this:

"So did we have any melting icebergs around here in the last three to five years?" one person asked.

"Sure," a second responded quickly.

"I think the most obvious one has to do with the satisfaction expressed from our clients. It wasn't as dramatic as with the penguins, where in a few months, things might have blown up. And that was a part of our problem. It was just going down and down so slowly for so many years that it was never dramatic or in anyone's face."

"But they had the same problem in the penguin story.

The iceberg had been melting so slowly that it was hard to recognize. So when somebody did point it out, there was the natural tendency to say—where's the proof? What are you talking about? To blame someone else for it or to make excuses. To say the little bit of downtick in customer satisfaction, or any relevant outcome, is just a matter of something that will go away soon. Or to say that you're just focusing on the negatives, that there are still many positive comments about the level of service."

"That's easy to see in retrospect. But at the time it was not."

"I think the biggest problem here was that the group had been so successful for so many years. It had a lot of pride and comfort."

"Was there a Fred?"

"Sure. Sullivan was a Fred. And Tammy as well."

"True, but I think they got whacked a few times and just backed down. I'm not criticizing them, since I think the whacks probably felt pretty hard."

"But isn't the point here, or the bigger point, that it can be awfully easy, just as with the penguins, to miss the melting or reject warning voices, if it happens slowly or not in a dramatic way?"

[Note from Holger and John: See how the "iceberg" language actually facilitates conversation.]

Case 2: Don't just go with who you have. Go with who you need.

Here's another small example, from a different meeting in a different place and time:

"Has anyone seen any examples of significant changes that were particularly successful?"

"I'd say Cara's group was remarkably successful in making a lot happen, about two years ago, and in a very short period. And, as we know, it worked out very well."

"I agree."

"So how did they do it?"

"At least a part of their success had to do with the group who drove the changes."

"What do you mean?"

"Cara was sort of a Louis. Her Alice was George Karter."

"And she had a Fred. Maybe more than one."

"Song was one. He was a relatively new employee, full of ideas, sometimes a bit naive, but amazingly creative."

"And Tim had a lot of the Professor in him."

"And Rodriguez was much like Buddy."

"Did she pick them out as deliberately as the Head Penguin did?"

No one knew.

"And knowing Cara, I bet she didn't just tell them they were now on the new IT transformation task force. I bet she talked to them individually, and made it clear that if someone felt they were too busy or already sponsoring too many other initiatives, or whatever, they should decline. Her inclination would have been to only have a team that wanted to be there and therefore have the drive and inclination to do whatever it would take to succeed. Which is what the Head Penguin did."

"Yes."

One person in the room looked at the person who just said yes and asked, "Which of the characters is most like you?"

"Me?"

"Yes."

"What do you think?"

"I'd say 70 percent Fred and 30 percent Buddy."

A few people nodded.

"Do we have any people behaving like a NoNo in our group?"

Almost everyone immediately looked at one of the people in the room. He saw this and said, "I'm not *that* bad!"

[Note from Holger and John: Never underestimate the power of genuine laughter, not cynical asides, to reduce stress and defensiveness, and to foster important conversations that might be difficult to have.]

Case 3: And the killer number one of any change is . . . ?

Here is one more snippet of a conversation. Again, different time and place and organization:

"What's been the biggest failure of a change initiative any of you have seen here?"

"For me, that's an easy question. It's the Jump Forward project."

About half the people in that room nodded quickly.

"So why was it such a failure?"

"I think they never developed any real sense of urgency. They just set up a project office. They came up with a plan. People were given parts of the plan to execute. But I doubt if half the people saw the point or the importance. Some thought it was a mistake. Some were just too busy to give it much attention. So even though the project office worked hard, I suspect it got bogged down pretty quickly."

"Did anyone really try to develop any sense of urgency?"

"If they did, there was nothing like the whole Coke bottle episode, or the ice sculpture, or that emotional speech from Louis or a Heroes Day that helped to win over the skeptics."

"I think they did put out some kind of communication early on about why some significant changes were needed. But it wasn't much. It was basically a memo from the boss. Maybe some cascading of other notices, but, as you said, nothing remotely like what the penguins did."

"I think communication was a problem through-out the effort. There is nothing like posters underneath the iceberg where the penguins swam almost every day. There was no relentless effort, or a lot of people helping, or much of anything."

"There had to be project report updates."

"No doubt, but I bet it was just to the people in charge of the department, not to any of the hundreds of others who were in one way or another being affected or whose help would have made a difference."

"He's right. I didn't see anything."

"And they certainly had few, or certainly not enough, enthusiastic volunteers like Amanda, the scouts, or the kindergartener Sally Ann."

[Note from Holger and John: Never underestimate the importance of a real sense of urgency felt by many, many people.]

Case 4: Change that doesn't sustain itself is not change.

One last example:

"The implementation of the new go-to-market strategy was successful by all the metrics they used. But I doubt if anyone today would say, if they were being objective and looked at how we actually do go to market and the results we are getting, that the success has sustained itself. Maybe we have moved a bit in the right direction, or a promising direction. But compared to a few years ago . . ."

"We are back closer to the way we had always done things over there."

"So what went wrong?"

"Well, think about the penguins. What did they do that was different?"

"A lot more of them were into the game and with some enthusiasm. A lot more than in our case developed that sense of urgency, a lot more bought into what was happening, and a lot more actually were involved in making the big change happen because they wanted to. They 'volunteered.'"

"I think in our case there was some up-front selling with a business case."

"I remember a thick stack of PowerPoints."

"I don't."

"No, there was. But after that it was just a matter of putting the initiatives into the operating plan and budget and holding people accountable."

"But we do that all the time and it works."

"No, we do that to accomplish more or less routine work or small improvements. And that seems to work. Here we are talking about a much more fundamental change."

"So the distinction between routine and small improvements versus a bigger shift is important?"

"I think so. And that deserves some discussion here. Think for a minute about what the Chicago office did . . ."

[Note from Holger and John: When you are considering any

sort of initiative that demands change, think (hard) about how many people will need to alter what they do. As the numbers grow, the issue becomes large-scale change, which requires a different process than small scale.]

You get the idea?

We have seen an initial conversation lead to other conversations and to more productive conversations. More thoughtful. More informed. Less defensive. With fewer misunderstandings about what people are saying, because they have a shared reference point and language.

We have found that an initial discussion can begin with a bit of awkwardness on the surface—since here is a serious group of adults talking about a silly fable! This can lead to nervous laughter (but laughter is not bad!) or to the person feeling the most threatened by the conversation trying to shut it down. But all it takes is one or two brave souls to ask or answer the quite rational questions, and these discussions take off.

We urge you to try it!

The End

(except for readers wanting extra credit)

Q&A with the Authors

Question: Why have you done a tenth anniversary edition of *Our Iceberg Is Melting*?

John Kotter: For me, there are two reasons. First, in the last ten years the world has continued to shift in some important ways, and it seems a shame not to have some of that commentary in the book. And second, we've learned a lot from discussions with people who have used the book over the last decade—about how they think that it has been helpful to them, and I want to have that information for our current readers.

Question: So what have you learned in the last decade?

JK: The most basic point is that the rate of change continues to go up in most places, in most industries, and in most sectors. As a result, the number of significant initiatives inside organizations has gone up. Initiatives in operations, marketing, sales, finance, anywhere. And that has big implications.

Holger Rathgeber: For example, if you walk around today and randomly ask, "Who of you is involved in some form of change at work?" No matter whether you are in a management meeting, a sales conference, or on the packing line of a manufacturer—the number of raised hands has grown over the past decade to be very, very impressive. And, literally, most of us, in my opinion, are not prepared for this reality, at least not to the degree necessary.

We throw people into launching and supporting change initiatives and projects and we just assume that life and past experiences have been a good teacher for everybody to pick up today's relevant insights and skills. But we have seen again and again that this is not necessarily true when you have to change more often and in bigger ways. Life—which means the past—can be a pretty bad teacher.

And I think that is where this story has such a huge

importance because it helps you to find language and orientation in moments where there's confusion around what could we do, what should we do, and what must we do. In this story there is at least a process. The process is based on real research and countless real-life situations we have encountered; it is clear—not easy to do, but clear. It's usually helpful in moments where you look around and most of the people are confused and our story has, in its simple core, a sequence of actions that raises the probability of you and your team succeeding not just by a small margin, but by a significant margin.

That's why we wrote this book in the first place. That's why we are launching it with new insights. I am convinced it is even more relevant and important than it was ten years ago.

Question: Have you changed the story?

JK: Loyal readers, who use this book on a regular basis with others, I suspect won't even notice some subtle things that we changed. It's almost like—in shooting a movie, you shoot a lot more film than actually goes into the movie. So imagine if a director, ten years later, goes back with all the feedback that he's gotten from audiences and does a new "director's cut." To make the film an even more powerful experience for audiences. And maybe he or she even takes into account how society has been changing since the film was originally produced. Again to make it more powerful today. So some lines or short scenes that didn't make it into the original are added. Maybe a few lines are cut out. Small shifts but very purposeful. The story is still the story, but hopefully more powerful given what we have learned and given the renewed urgency of learning how to negotiate change. That is sort of what has happened here.

HR: Here is an example. In the more rapidly changing world of today, we often find initiatives in firms that are somewhat bigger than a decade ago. Bigger leaps. With larger goals and everything happening faster, it is even more difficult at the start to say exactly what will be changed. There is more uncertainty, which can produce more anxiety. So we made a small change in the story to reflect one way we have seen people deal well with this reality.

Think about when Louis goes out in front of the group, saying that the iceberg is melting and they need to do something. Without having the solution at hand or even in mind, obviously, there's quite a few people who move from "everything is fine" into panic, into fear, which is almost as insidious as the ignorance of "there's a problem." So in this edition we have Buddy and others talk to those whose troubled minds block them from doing anything. It's a small change—a new paragraph—but not an unimportant point.

Question: You [Kotter] have been doing research on organizational performance, particularly in a changing world, and the leadership needed to drive good performance, for decades. Almost exclusively you have published the results in professional books written for managers. Here you chose something very different, a fable. Why?

JK: I've been studying for a long time how people learn. And I think it is pretty clear that our brains are hard-wired for stories. A good story is easy to absorb and remember, especially if it has emotional components.

This is probably because that was how humans learned for tens of thousands of years. The leader tells the youngsters the great story about how one from their clan grabbed dinner from the mouth of the saber-toothed tiger and saved the tribe, or how he was eaten by the saber-toothed tiger. A dramatic, interesting story that has important lessons in it.

One form of story is the animal fable. It has the advantage of being short and it is appealing to a much wider range of people than traditional management books. If it's done well, with interesting animals doing unusual things, it can be striking and particularly memorable. And good fables have some basic points in them that, because they stick around in your mind, can actually change what we do.

So, I was thinking about and talking to people about the whole idea of taking important management lessons and put them into fable form when Holger came along with a great idea.

HR: The whole thing started when I was asked to spend two to three hours with a large audience of managers and executives focusing on John's Eight Steps from his *Leading Change* book. It was clear to me that a PowerPoint presentation wasn't a good way to do this. So I created a very rough plot about a colony of penguins sitting on an iceberg that is melting. They encounter typical challenges and go through the Eight Steps. The story was a highly simplified version of what we eventually wrote. But. . . .

JK: And Holger sent me a brief email telling me about what he had done. And I thought it was immensely creative. I loved it. One thing led to another and about a year later I said: let's write a book.

Question: So is this fable based on your research and real-life stories you have studied?

JK: Yes. I don't even know how far back you have to go to see the whole trail of that work. Certainly thirty years, maybe more. We've learned more in the last decade too.

Question: Recent research is reflected in this new edition?

JK: Yes. We have learned, for example, that talking about hazards, like your iceberg is melting, is a great way to catch people's attention if they're very complacent. But if you keep hitting them with hazard, hazard, hazard, they panic, and panic doesn't help people. They start worrying about themselves or their families, not the community, and anxiety can start to wear them down. There's a lot of evidence that's come up in the last decade that to sustain any effort to make some big changes that are needed you have to shift the emphasis from hazard to opportunity. You have to think more in positive terms. And this helps a group of people not to burn out, not to focus just on themselves, but to stay motivated and focused on the group. So, that's one example.

HR: Here is a second. In a world that is changing faster and faster, the number of people who have to get involved to give you the horsepower, so to speak, to deal with all of the big changes and at a speed that matches what's needed, the number of people who have to be proactively engaged is going up, not by increments, but factors. And our traditional methods of dealing with this aren't able to produce that level of broad-based action and commitment. Putting the changes on the same few people around you is a mistake and doesn't work.

You need a larger group to drive it, or at least more people helping the core group. Communication has always been important. But if more people get involved and have to be involved you need more and continuous communication to keep everybody into it. You need to broadcast information about successes to keep people on board and build credibility. And you need to constantly broadcast where you want and need help to set the compass for creative solutions and initiatives of many people that actually pay into the vision and not just produce more activity.

Question: Why did you choose penguins as your characters?

HR: John's original *Leading Change* book about the Eight Steps already had penguins on the cover. So there is no doubt it influenced our decision. Another reason, simply put, is that penguins, particularly emperor penguins, are fascinating creatures that for mysterious reasons we humans can easily relate to and that can put a smile on our faces, all of which is very helpful.

Question: Is there one takeaway you want readers to carry with them?

JK: Yes. In these turbulent times, sufficient leadership, not just from the top couple of people, is very important, far too rare, and it does not have to be that way. It often starts with only one person not looking away or waiting for something to happen, but seizing opportunities to act where others see problems, fault or threat. Why couldn't that one person be you, or anyone reading this interview right now?

HR: And then it's all about teamwork—aligned leadership. The Eight Steps are a good guide to figure out what the work is, when it involves change, which, frankly, is the case most of the time now.

Question: Have you thought about *Our Iceberg Is Melting 2,* a real sequel, not just this tenth anniversary edition?

JK: We have. We've talked about it, and who knows, in the future, we might still do it. But our minds struggled with how to do an extension of this. So we said, let's start from scratch, and Holger's creative mind started looking around for other story lines and animals and we actually landed on something. It's a line that goes beyond the process of change and examines the underlying forces based on our newest research. And we picked this time—or Holger did and I agreed—meerkats.

HR: These cute little animals that you find in Africa. And the name of the book is *That's Not How We Do It Here!* Great fun to write and we're already receiving evidence that people are finding it useful.

JK: Which, of course, is very gratifying. All of my research and, in a sense, my lifework leaves me utterly convinced that the study and practice of leadership and change will become even more important in the future and an essential skill for all of you who want to help create it.

The Authors

John Kotter, often called the world's foremost authority on leadership and change, is an award-winning Harvard Business School emeritus professor of leadership, a *New York Times* bestselling author, and cofounder of the consulting firm, Kotter International.

Holger Rathgeber is a former Fortune 500 executive, a regular collaborator with Kotter—most recently on *That's Not How We Do It Here!*—and a principal at Kotter International.

Kotter International is a new breed of consulting firm that unlocks the full power of an organization to achieve sustainable strategic results faster than leaders believe possible, while building cultures that are agile and quick as well as reliable and efficient.

Visit us at **www.kotterinternational.com** for more resources and case studies of real organizations (not penguin colonies).

If you loved *Our Iceberg Is Melting*, you'll also love . . .

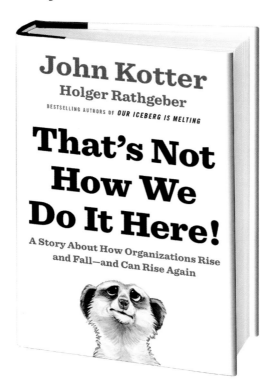

"This unique parable shows us how we're *safer* in changing times when we innovate!" **—Spencer Johnson, MD, author of *Who Moved My Cheese?***

"This simple parable of furry mammals facing the challenge of adapting to threat offers real insights into the journey so many of us must make. Brilliant!" **—General Stanley McChrystal, retired, author of *Team of Teams* and cofounder of the McChrystal Group**

"John Kotter does it again. His use of metaphor helps readers distill down to the fundamental requirements for a high-performing organization: tapping the hearts and minds of team members in service to a compelling purpose." **—Leigh Morgan, COO, Bill and Melinda Gates Foundation**

ISBN 9780399563942
www.kotterinternational.com/books